messages from my self DREAMS

by Ruth Kramer

with illustrations by
Stanley C. Whitehead

CELESTIAL ARTS
MILLBRAE, CALIFORNIA 94030

Copyright © 1973 by Celestial Arts
231 Adrian Road, Millbrae, California 94030

No part of this book may be reproduced by any mechanical, photographic, or electronic process, or in the form of a phonographic recording, nor may it be stored in a retrieval system, transmitted, or otherwise copies for public or private use without the written permission of the publisher.

First Printing, August 1973
Library of Congress Card No.:73-82535
ISBN: 0-912310-33-2 Paper Edition
Made in the United States of America

Introduction

by

Virginia Satir

World Renown Lecturer
and Family Therapist

Author of "Conjoint Family Therapy"
and "People Making"

I see in my dreams an effort on my part to make some new sense about myself—they are a dialogue between myself and me. My dreams are mine; I dreamed them up all by myself. But what are they trying to say to me?

Only I can know. Dream interpretations are often thought of as being the province of the mystic or psychiatrist. The real expert is the dreamer himself. People often tell me their dreams and ask me what they mean. "I cannot tell you," I say. "They are your dreams. You have the key."

Just as in my waking life—where I see myself responding in ways that puzzle, surprise, and scare or delight me—my night eye offers a myriad of experiences. I often feel like

Columbus, sailing around in unknown seas, quite sure that something is there, but not knowing exactly what.

It always turns out that something <u>is</u> there, if I am willing to explore far enough and deep enough. Over the centuries countless people have undertaken this adventure. Whether their interpretations are "right" or "wrong" they have always been beguiled by the mystery inherent in the stories of their dreams.

Through "Dreams: Messages from My Self" Ruth Kramer can help many of us gain new insights into this mystery. In a simple but dynamic way she has added a dimension that makes it possible to view our dreams so that they will further enrich our lives.

From my self to my self . . .

Oh, the dreamer
the beautiful dreamer
gazing upward to the beautiful sky . . .
listening to the world —
Oh life — you are so beautiful!

We all dream
from primitive man to modern man
for our instincts and fundamental desires
are essentially alike.
There are levels of the personality
which unite all of us.
The primitive, biological, unconscious.

Traditionally, a dream is defined as a state of consciousness during sleep. Tracing the word DREAM, we find the root meaning in a German word, TRAUM, in turn related to a German verb TRÜGEN, meaning to "deceive"; however, in relating to dreams this probably comes closer to veiling. A unique process begins when we go to sleep; a new language comes forth, a symbolic or picture language with secret codes — it is the communication from ourselves to ourselves. The symbols are the clues and the key to understanding that part of ourself called the unconscious.

One of the essential characteristics of dreams is that they are our own invention, drawn completely from our various parts. A dream is ours; We create the plot and assign ourselves a role within it. The pictures we see are our own symbols expressing our inner sensory experience. These symbols are the messengers from our intuitive self to our rational self.

One of the essential characteristics of dreams is that they are our own invention, drawn completely from our various parts. A dream is ours; we create the plot and assign ourselves a role within it. The pictures we see are our own symbols expressing our inner sensory experience. These symbols are the messengers from our intuitive self to our rational self.

The symbols of primitive cultures and more highly developed cultures are strikingly similar because they delve into sensory and emotional experiences known by all people.

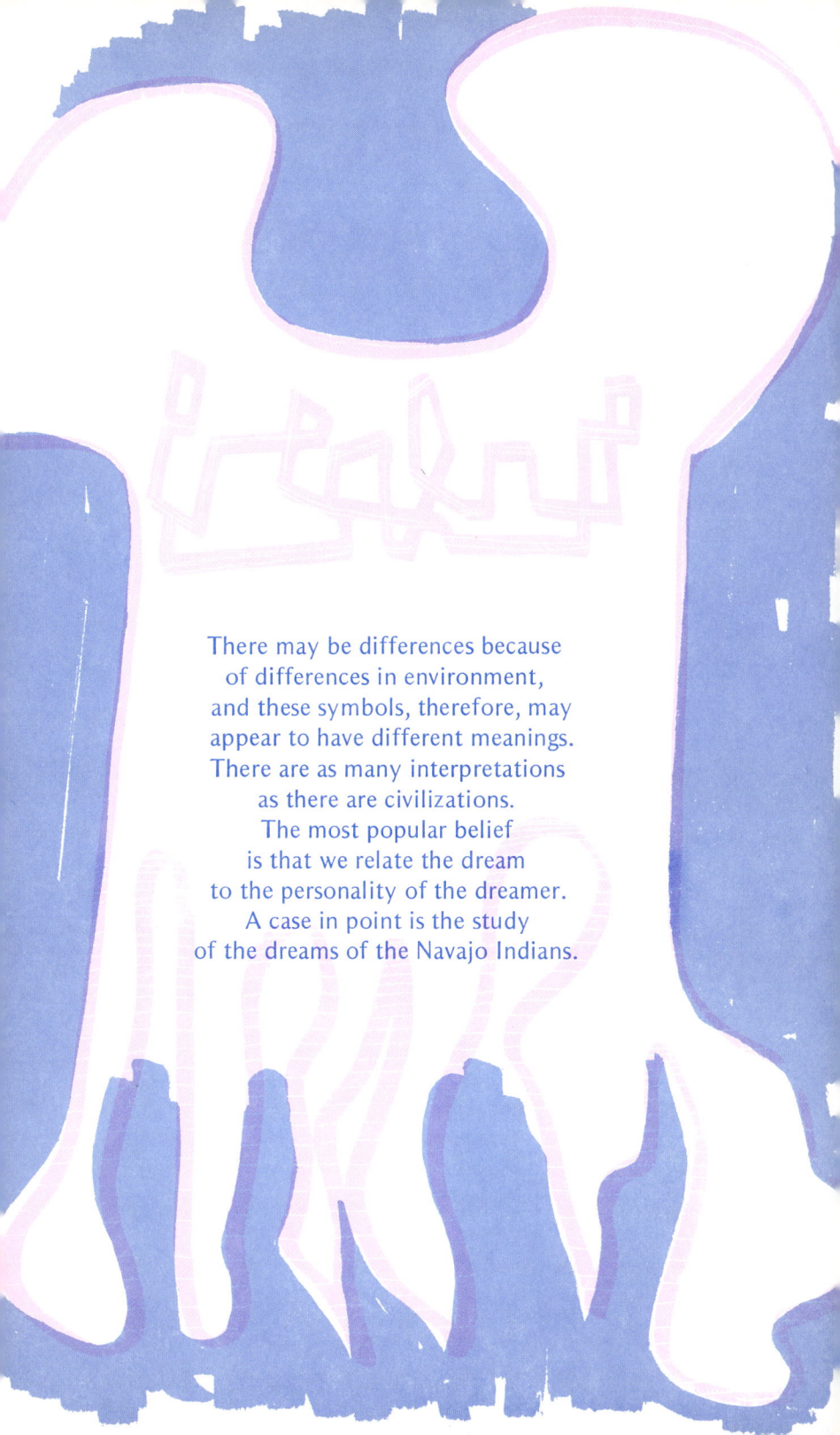

There may be differences because
of differences in environment,
and these symbols, therefore, may
appear to have different meanings.
There are as many interpretations
as there are civilizations.
The most popular belief
is that we relate the dream
to the personality of the dreamer.
A case in point is the study
of the dreams of the Navajo Indians.

Many of us say "I never dream," yet scientific experiments have proven that everyone dreams. While we are asleep another world becomes alive. There we experience various stages of sleep; one being the dream-sleep stage. Experimental studies are continuously being made with the use of an electroencephalograph, commonly called an EEG machine. The brain patterns are traced by attaching a group of wires to the head of a sleeping subject. At the end of these wires are small discs that act like sensitive microphones. When they are taped to the subject's head, tiny emissions of electricity from the brain is traced with automatic pens. During the rapid eye movement stage (REM) we dream—approximately every 90 minutes, and have from 3 to 9 dreams nightly; each dream lasting up to about 20 minutes.

Some of us remember our dreams better than others—it takes some training and a desire to remember. Sometimes our messages are painful. Normally one would want to forget a nightmare, but the message is very important. Perhaps it is a warning of the "nightmare" life we are leading.

On the other hand our dreams can reveal great wisdom and can be a powerful motivating force. We have the best and the worst in us. Usually our dreams express the mental activity which has been influenced during the day and our own personal reactions to them.

Tests have been made which deprive humans, as well as animals, of their dream sleep. When we fail to get enough sleep we become irritable, tense and anxious; have difficulty concentrating, show loss of memory, become fatigued, etc. When deprived for longer periods, hallucination and delirium occur.

Some of us dream in color,
but usually we dream in gray;
pictorially rather than linguistically.
If we are blind,
we do not have visual imagery
(unless previously sighted),
and if we are deaf,
we have no auditory imagery
(unless we once had hearing).

Although there are many viewpoints about dreams,
widely recognized authorities
such as Freud, Jung and Fromm
agree that dreams are the main path
to the understanding of the unconscious,
the key to the restoration
of our psychological balance.

The advancement of the scientific age
has discouraged us
from looking inward for our own reality.
Instead, we project our hopes,
wishes and fears
onto the outside world.

Almost always
the dream reflects
some unfinished business;
it continuously recurs
for us to solve.

Our creative energies are blocked and sapped by our neurotic behavior. By day we use tremendous amounts of energy covering up, pushing back, denying, repressing aspects of ourselves which we do not want to accept.

Instead of possessing our own thoughts and fantasies, we project them onto others, assigning others our own creativity.

Many creative and celebrated people
have used dream material and fantasies.
To name only a few:
Anaïs Nin, extremely popular today
for her beautiful, colorful writings,
kept a diary and tells
the importance of her dream life
in her work.
William Blake is famous
for his symbolic poetry and art.
Salvador Dali is noted for his surrealist,
dream-like paintings.
Robert Louis Stevenson used
his dreams
for some of his best romances,
and the plot for Dr. Jekyll
and Mr. Hyde was revealed to him in a dream.
The well-known poem Kubla Khan,
written by William Coleridge,
came to him in a dream.
As he wrote the poem word for word
he was interrupted.
This broke his train of thought,
so he completed it
on another level of his mind,
the conscious.
Richard Bach, author
of Jonathan Livingston Seagull,
had set aside the original,
incomplete story for years,
when one morning he awoke
from a strange dream
of seagulls and quickly completed his story.

What is missing in our lives?
Our dreams tell us about our projections—
of the other parts played out in drama,
sometimes heavy and bizarre.

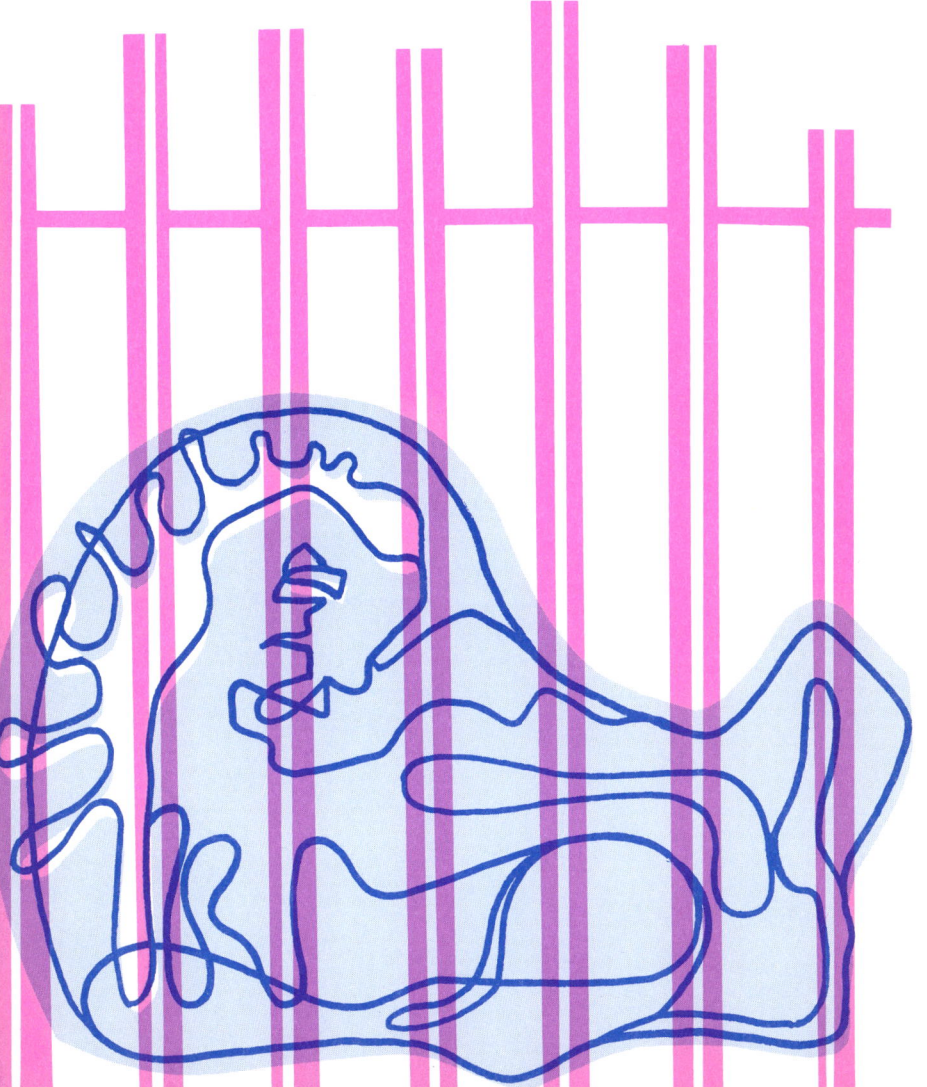

During the day we have scattered information
coming in to our organism,
but we are often too busy or frightened
to be aware of it—
so at night when we are at rest
our brain weaves the information together
and comes up with a picture story.

In our dreams
we meet many of our parts
which we have "cast" aside
during the day,
especially the parts of ourselves
we call
"evil,
wicked,
horrible,
terrifying,
scary,
low,
rotten,
etc."
We say they do not belong to us.

Until we understand ourselves and begin to link the unconscious with the conscious, we look to others to "define" us. Usually nonverbally, we say, "Be a credit to us, children, so others can say how wonderful we are" ... our lovers must tell us how lovable we are, our friends to cheer us when we are depressed instead of understanding the depression. We are constantly asking others to be our missing aspects of ourselves—to fill in the "holes" in our personalities.

We are afraid of the dark, shadowy, bogey-man side, and many of us project this onto the black man instead of owning it and becoming friends with ourselves. By keeping down the shadow which is constantly asking for recognition, we allow ourselves to become plastic, hollow, and superficial.

"It is mere self-love to be inconsolable at seeing one's own imperfections."

—Fenelon

Once we begin to listen
we can understand the need
for integrating these disowned aspects
in order to become whole human beings.
Hate and fear
can be transformed
into useful potentialities—
creation comes from conflict.

"A man must have chaos yet within him
 to give birth to a dancing star"—
                              Nietzsche

By understanding our deep,
dark, opposite side
we learn to love
the crippled, misfit, broken child
in ourselves . . . .
which unloved makes us sick
and loved makes us grow.

"Come, said my Soul,
Such verses for my Body
let us write, (for we are one)
That should I after death
invisibly return,
Or long, long hence,
in other spheres.

"There to some group of mates
the chants resuming,
(Tallying Earth's soul, trees,
winds, tumultuous waves,)
Ever with pleas'd smile
I may keep on,
Ever and ever yet
the verses owning—
as, first, I here and now,
Signing for Soul and Body,
set to them my name."
—Walt Whitman

WE ACT OUT

in our dreams
our unresolved emotional conflicts.
There we set up the stage,
the actors, props.
There we feel the pain,
anxiety, frustrations, sadness,
grief we can't face during the day.
But until we solve the conflicts,
they keep insisting for a resolution.

"Let life happen to you; believe me, life is right"
—Rilke

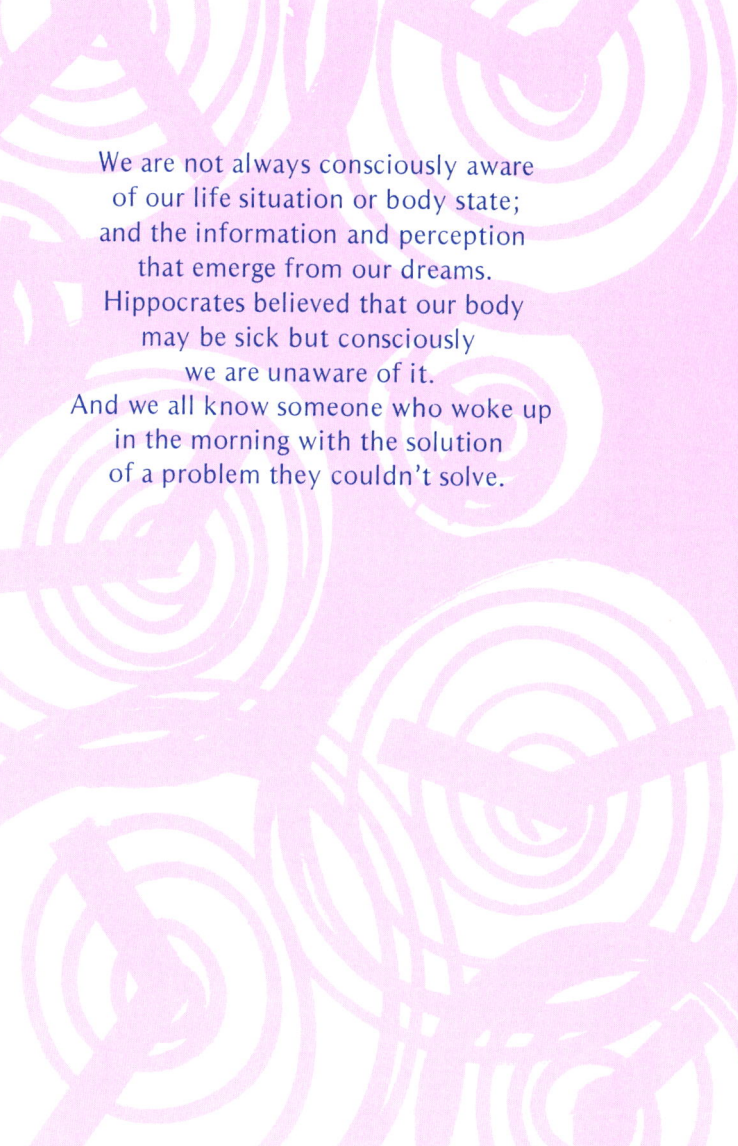

We are not always consciously aware
of our life situation or body state;
and the information and perception
that emerge from our dreams.
Hippocrates believed that our body
may be sick but consciously
we are unaware of it.
And we all know someone who woke up
in the morning with the solution
of a problem they couldn't solve.

The task of living from birth on is to seek our wholeness—our center.

Understanding and using our dreams is a rich avenue for that search.

The path to self-acceptance,
to self-knowledge; the way
of life itself — these involve
directions, implications
you will not always be aware of.
To find sources, origins,
trust the path,
the way of the dream.

Dreams are one means to transcend.
A beginning
to the discovery
of our secret wisdom.

The dream pictures
are symbols of something we feel.
We are all different,
therefore,
our symbols are individualized.
Water can mean one thing to me,
and another to you.

Let yourself fully see your dream.
Don't overlook anything.
Ask yourself some questions.
Where does the dream take place, why there?
Who was in the dream?
For what purpose?
What happens in the dream?
What emotions did you feel?
An insignificant thing may be relevant.

Let's look closer

at the opposite sex in our dreams.

We need to become more in touch

with our opposites—

for now it is widely accepted

that we have both male and female

components

in ourselves.

The Chinese philosophy of Yin and Yang
beautifully describes the relationships
of these opposites.
Yin is the element of rest, unaltering,
the moist, the female, the dark, the cool,
the mountainside in shade.
Yang is the element of movement and change,
the dry, the male, the bright, the hot
the mountainside in sun.
Yin endlessly moves towards Yang,
Yang endlessly moves towards Yin.
Yin is the seed of Yang.
Yang contains the seed of Yin.
Yin endlessly becomes Yang.
Yang perpetually becomes Yin —
the two, the entire work together
in harmony for those who see the opposite
in their deep, chosen compliance
with the laws of Heaven.

One night I had a splendid dream
where I met my man within.
He asked me to dance
and what a dance!
The dream took place in a strange land
and I had never met him before.
Yet we danced as though we were one—
fantastic movements, unbelievable splits.
I was so flexible,
it was like I was a rubber band.
This is a good example of the combination
of our male-female parts harmonizing.

Too often we keep our male and female parts at war.

Try something for yourself.
With your notebook and pen at your bedside,
go to sleep telling yourself
you will remember your dream.
Upon waking,
write down your dream in the present tense . . .

here's one of my examples.

I'm in the back yard and H . . . and I are looking at this tall, beautiful tree—a tomato tree. It is a solid, strong tree loaded with large, bright, juicy tomatoes. There are no leaves, I notice, only ripe, heavy fruit. H . . . is gleefully picking them while I am urging him to pick only those we can eat now . . . to leave the others on the tree for us to enjoy until we need them.

P.S. Put a date on your dream.

If you would like to go more deeply,
try to connect something that happened
that day to stimulate the dream.
You might find it helpful
to paint a picture of your dream
or let it manifest itself
in an art form.
You might also want to take
one person or thing in the dream
and try to bring it to life
through a dialogue method which I will explain later.

To deepen your understanding of your dream, take another step and let yourself come in touch with the mood you feel in your dream. Usually after writing and drawing, some of the feelings will begin to stir, if they haven't jumped out already. As I drew the tomato tree, I felt an awe and a wonder looking at this very solid, fruit-laden tree, but also an uneasiness—for there were no leaves anywhere! What comes to mind is that I've been very, very busy in my life producing, creating, using vast amounts of energy. These tomatoes certainly were and could be the fruits of my labors—yet, when they're picked there seems to be no evidence of any future growth. I get the message that I'd better start digging at the roots, fertilizing, giving loving care to this tree of life, ME!

As you go along,
let yourself be aware
of what your symbols mean to you.
This can be fun sometimes.

I can start by asking myself, "How come tomatoes, why not peaches, cherries, apples, etc.?" "Why does this tree not have leaves, and what does it mean that the tree is tall, solid, sturdy?"

Now you might try a dialogue with some of the parts,
particularly those in conflict or which are distasteful.
Be the one part, talking to the other,
then reverse parts. Here is an example
of my dialogue:

Tree: I am a tall, solid tree with several very heavy ripe fruit waiting to be picked. I feel until they are picked from me, I can't grow any more. I have to concentrate very hard to hold on to them or they'll fall and be smashed.

Tomato: I'm so big and full of juice. I need someone to pick me and use me. I can't become smaller and go back to what I once was—a seed and I can't get much larger and juicier for my skin isn't able to contain any more. I'm looking hopefully at Ruth and she looks hesitant -- but I see H... willing to take me.

Ruth: You are so beautiful to look at. I can't bear to pick all of you and leave a bare tree. You might not grow back again, in fact, I know you'll never grow back again in this same form and this makes me sad. Maybe different tomatoes will grow, but not the same, nothing will be the same—I want to hold on to what I can see. I don't like not knowing.

Tomato: If you don't pick me, I'll waste and if you pick me, you can enjoy me; either way, I'll be transformed into something else. You can't do any thing about it—it's the law of nature, living and dying.

As you look at a series of your dreams,
you can watch for a theme
which begins to emerge.
The time and place may be different
but there will be something
which has a sameness.
At the beginning of my exploration
into my dream life, I recorded
four dreams -- which follow
in sequence. In this series,
there is water and for me, in
this context, water is the
unconscious, the unknown.

I am standing, fully dressed, across much water;
someone asks me how I'm going to return
with all my clothes on.
I ask if there is another route that can be used
—there is another lake but I'm told
I can walk around it even tho it will take longer.
The water is clean, smooth and pretty.

Notice how reluctant I am to get into the water.
I inquire and find there is another way
to get around it even though it will take longer.
As I skirt the water I do speculate
on how clean, smooth and pretty the water is.

I am inside a patio or covering of some sort; there is a large pool, Grecian-like with a ledge covered with moss. It is old and slanting toward the water and the cement has broken away—I walk along this ledge, carefully—I wade a bit, then I am walking slowly, carrying in my hand an odd-shaped (pop-art-like) tray and on one end of it there is a plastic bowl, square-shaped. In the bowl is dirty, mossy water with strange shaped creatures—they are all black, some partly formed—some like tadpoles, others growing and developing right out of the water—somehow I know that this water once had beautiful fish but the water had not been changed and taken care of. . . I go outside to a spot near the pool where there is a small patch of moist grass and as I throw the contents of the bowl in to be rid of them, I realize that I'm throwing them in a moist-growing place and they'll continue to grow . . . .

I am still skirting the water by walking along the ledge, finally wade a bit. Next, I'm carrying a small vessel of water which reveals some of my dark, lurking creatures transforming and growing out of the water.

I'm in an enclosure which is round, glassed in, like an arboretum in a far away place ... there are many plants growing and a beautiful pool is in the center. Inside there is an eligible bachelor; who is tall and thin. Outside is another woman at the door trying to get in—the man almost "chose" her but chooses me. We are sitting at the pool, my feet dangling in the water . . . he begins making love to me—I begin to wake up— make myself go back to dream to get involved—I continue to wake up and force myself to go back to my dream

Here I am getting in touch with my masculine aspect which is beginning to emerge—but I haven't taken the full plunge yet.

I'm swimming underneath the water ...
there are fish in the water also as I swim in and around.
One of the fish brushes against my skin
and seems to sting me. When I come out of the water,
I notice that my arm doesn't hurt,
even though I've been stung.

Having become aware of my aggressive, decision-making male aspect, I am now swimming and exploring in and around.
The fish is associated with insights, knowledge and wisdom.
I'm not hurt as I've been brushed up against this side of my being.

Following the dream series of dipping into my unconscious

I'm in the process of selling old unwanted household things. In a large room I have tables set up with all the items, categorically arranged; old glasses, plates, cups, etc. I go out of the room, trusting people to leave the money. I go in from time to time and find many of the items have been sold—in some places completely cleaned out. Some change has been left in small bowls which I left for that purpose.

this dream came forth:

The old, unwanted household things are those parts of myself which I've begun to inspect, sort, rearrange, transform. The things I saw myself doing in my waking life began to take on different meaning and helped me consciously to more effectively influence my own life. So I let myself play with and understand the wonderful, puzzling, scary world of my night life. It might do the same for you.

Compulsive
Dependent-Clinger
Doubter
Angry
Resentful
Fragmented
Ambivalent
Ridiculer
Greedy

I have encountered some of my many parts in my dreams

Fearful
Distracter
Cowardly
Avoider
Neglectful
Prejudiced

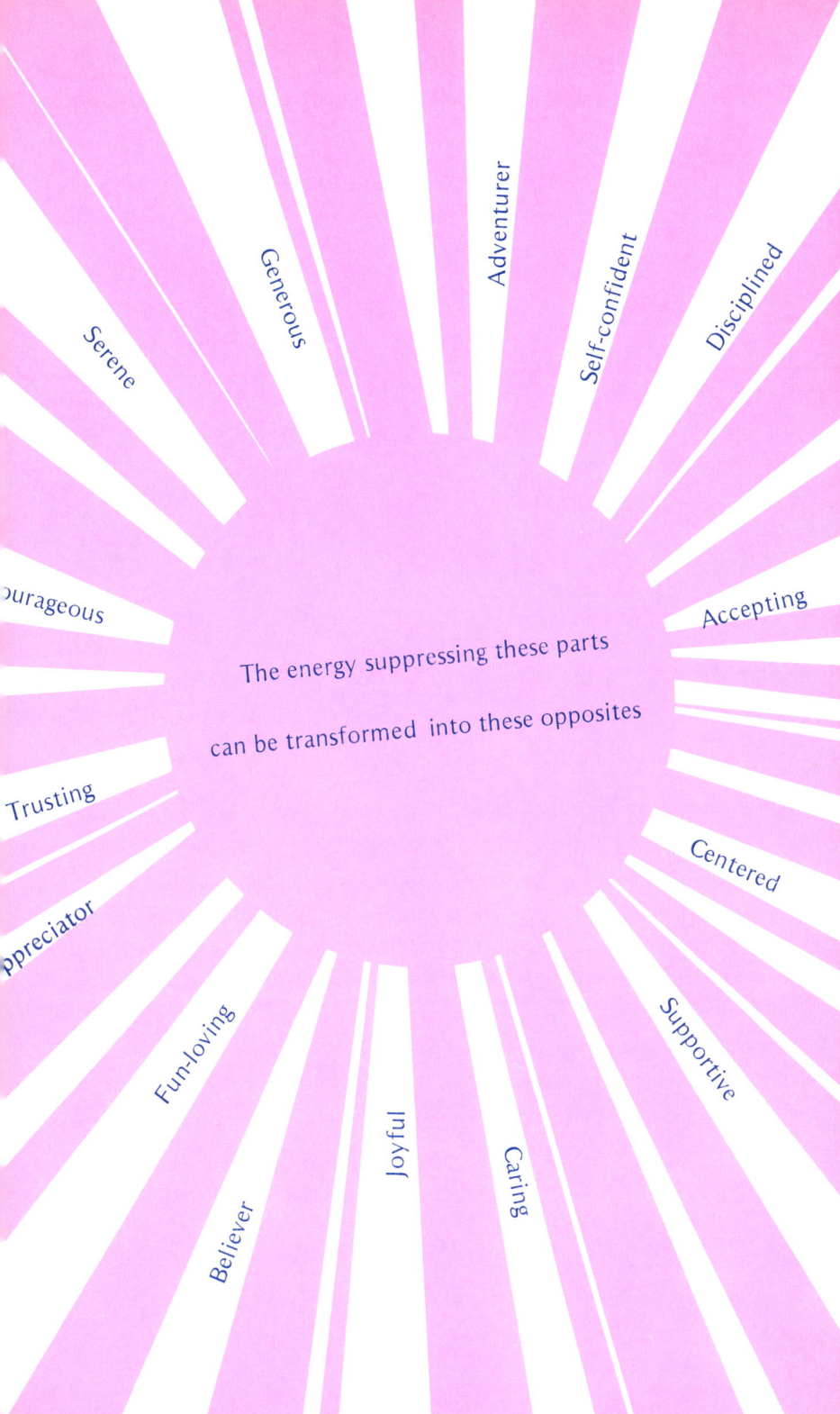

There's a road, there's a road, there's a journey which most of us promise (to ourselves) that we'll take (someday, but not now) and we fill ourselves with substitutes, avoiding, unyielding, procrastinating, Waiting, Hoping, Praying, Yearning for the other to do it for us . . .

How can we take this journey to ourselves?

The following dreams were very shocking, but eventually enlightening to me. The theme running through is that of a neglected child... and one very close to being snuffed out in one way or another. I came to realize the neglected child symbolized my creative essence, my soul, my only "real" life-part. As we all have a unique creative core, it's exciting to think about the "store house" of creative energies within each and everyone of us.

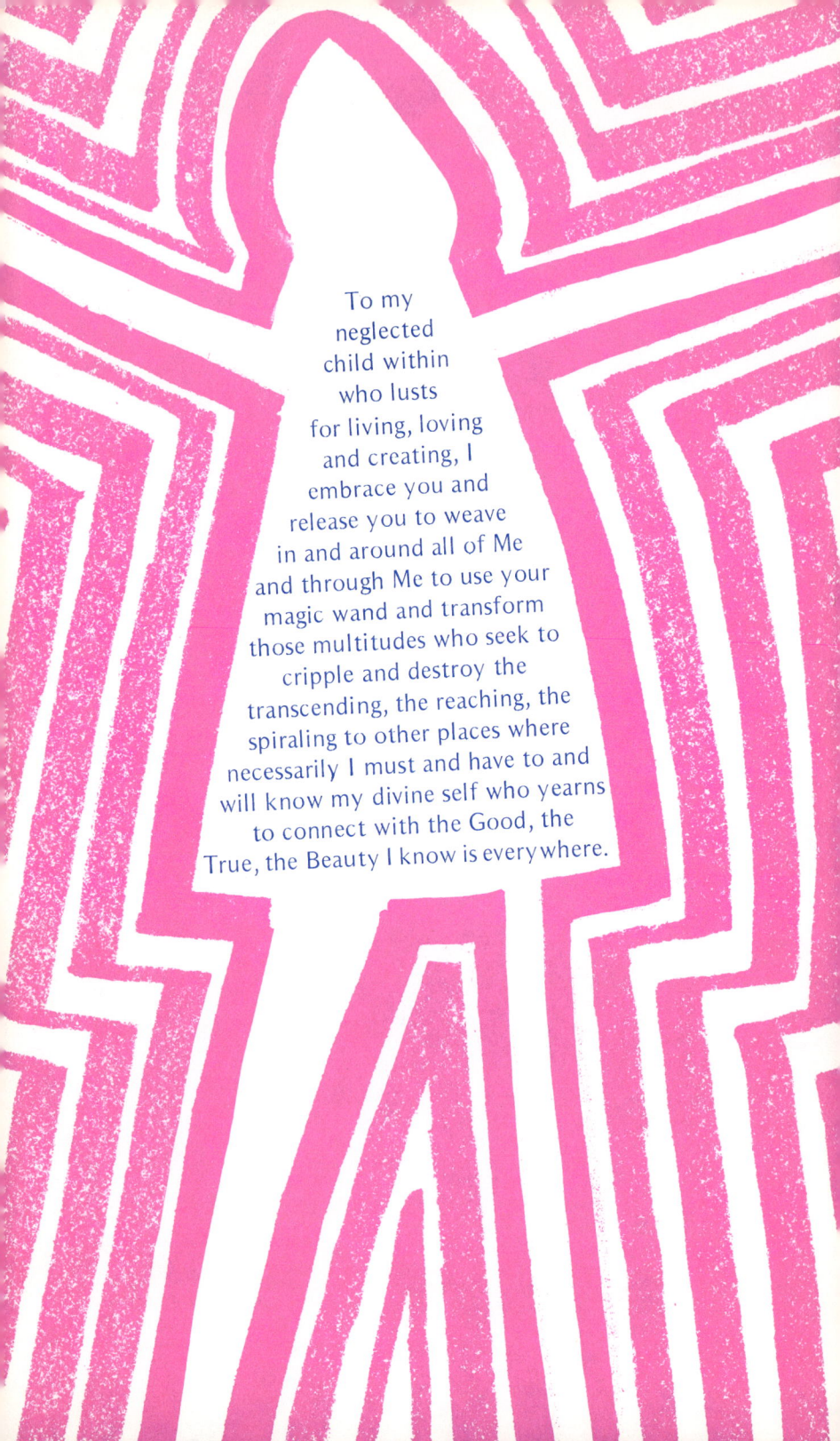

To my
neglected
child within
who lusts
for living, loving
and creating, I
embrace you and
release you to weave
in and around all of Me
and through Me to use your
magic wand and transform
those multitudes who seek to
cripple and destroy the
transcending, the reaching, the
spiraling to other places where
necessarily I must and have to and
will know my divine self who yearns
to connect with the Good, the
True, the Beauty I know is everywhere.

Dreams
Of my
"Neglected
 Child."

July 24

F--- is taking a woman into a classroom for a therapeutic session. She is sitting at a regular school desk; he's at the blackboard. The session is to solve a mystery for her husband is in Washington, D.C. and there are some secret orders or messages—later I talk to her about some missing brand-new brassieres which she now admits knowing something about (formerly denied). I am entering the classroom with M---, telling her all about F--- and the woman—I'm jealous that F--- was so friendly and helpful to her (I feel somehow I have second-best). I'm at the same desk as the woman. I have a small child with me, about two—she is sitting on my lap. I somehow have come to accept the responsibility of caring for her even tho it's cumbersome with her on my lap and I'm trying to learn. She sits with her back to me but leans way back to look at me. She is beautiful, strikingly so. Next, into the classroom comes the woman (who is the grandmother of child) and another woman (the mother). They are telling me they will watch and care for the child while I'm in the classroom. I go to the door with them and see the child running, fast towards the street (my anxiety is mounting for I know she'll be killed) I see a car coming—it runs over her... I look (as I'm screaming) towards the grandmother and she is laughing, sick-like. I see she is mad. I turn to the mother, and discover to my horror she is also mad. I am screaming to people walking across a wide street to please call an ambulance; people are unconcerned and walk by... I see the child getting up on hands and knees, she's very weak. She has grown, but I feel she's fatally injured.

August 18

　　　　　　　　　I am carrying a tiny baby about
and going to all sorts of places with some people.
　　　　　　I am very anxious to be included
　　　　　in what's going on. Now I turn around
and rush down the stairs with a mob of people.
　　　　　　　　　　　I have left my baby
　　　　　and she is tumbling down the stairs,
　　　　　　　　people trampling on her.
　　　She is helpless and trying to get down.
　　　　　　　　I rush over to pick her up,
　　　　　　　　know she is hurt and feel
I've done something which can't be undone.
　　　　　　　Except for this one occasion,
I have been taking care of my responsibility
　　　　　　　　even though it's a burden.
　　　　　　　　　　As I look at the baby
　　　　I see she looks like my mother's side
of the family and me. . .I'm owning it. . .
　　　　　　she is telling me I'm not making it
　　　　　as a responsible, nourishing person,
　　　that I'm merely doing the dutiful thing.

August 30

I'm in a house with a woman
who has some children of her own,
plus a boy and a girl she's raising. . .
I have the feeling she's a good, ideal mother,
relaxed, non-restrictive, non-up-tight.
I'm experiencing the house
as lived in, comfortable but not dirty.
I am comparing myself
with her and am envious. . .
someone has just told her that her little girl
had her arm caught in a neighbor's washing machine wringer—
she's calm, cool, collected—
she is remaining there, waiting
and I'm deeply concerned and anxious. . .
Now the foster daughter is acting up.
She's waiting for her dad to pick her up
and is counting on him. . .
she's yelling and I see her hopes are
in her Dad coming to get her. . .
He doesn't show up and she realizes
he's not going to. . .
she comes to me sobbing
and I take her in my arms and comfort her. . .
Now the small child comes in with badly hurt arms
and I hold her and suffer with her. . .

September 12

I'm taking care of a child-relative, about 4 or 5 years old—we are visiting old and sick relatives, people I haven't seen in years and showing the child to them. I want them to see and know the child who belongs to them—they are undesirables, ugly, sick, old, etc. Somehow I feel some closeness or pride in this task I chose to do. The last relative we visit lives in a big house. The child has a balloon and she loses it somehow and is crying about it; then falls in a square, well-like sewer. As I see her disappearing in the water, I think to myself, "I can't jump in to save her" for I feel this well has no bottom, it's a no-return, it's sure death. . . but immediately I jump in—I can't find her, I go down, down and finally, to my surprise, there is the bottom, but all that is there is wet, mossy leaves and garbage-like debris which I uncover with my hands. The space around me is small but the child is not there and I can't understand where she could have gone—I go up and awake.

September 29

I'm in the kitchen;
it's been raining and now getting dark.
All of a sudden I remember
the twin babies I've been taking care of
(I think they are grandchildren);
they are in the back yard
where I put them to get the sun,
under the trees and flowers.
With dread, I'm yelling to J.
"Quick, hurry, bring the babies in."
He rushes out and brings both babies in,
one under each arm.
I'm looking at them with remorse . . .
they had been out in just diapers to benefit from the sun
but now after all day in the cold, wet weather
one looks half-dead, the arm is stuck back,
I have left him too long.
I'm picking him up feeling
he will die and the baby is whispering
something like "It's too late."

October 2

J. is running late for school—his friends have come by the house to get him to come with them—they are hippies, drug users who play in a band. They pretend like they're not interested but I know they will not take J. to school. I prepare to drive him to make sure he goes, but I also have to go to school and I'm not ready. I have a baby and it needs to be changed and to be cared for. We all go in the car including my husband who is G. We arrive at school and drop J. off. I'm late for school, the baby is soaked and we have brought no provisions for it during the day with a sitter. He refuses to do anything and carelessly handles the baby—I'm afraid he'll drop it down an opening he's near— it's obvious the baby is a burden and I am torn between the needs of the baby and my own.

October 16

        I've entered a lobby of some sort—
       there is a small child sitting on the floor.
          The blinds have been drawn,
      it's almost dark, yet the middle of day—
apparently it's nap or quiet time for the child—
she is playing, sleepily on the floor with a toy.
             I lean over to her
and find she's weary, very sad, wet and neglected.
        This immediately overwhelms me
           and I feel sick with empathy.
            I pick her up, carry her
        to another part of the building,
and altho I'm busy I begin to care for her.
            I have places to go
and a schedule to attend to but she's very tired
       so I lie her down and reassure her
            I won't leave her alone—
      I change my plans and stay with her.

In the midst of the worldly dash of fragmented, busy, busy people. . .

I have watched and wanted and dreamed of the neglected child part of myself—the creative, loving, center, spiritual renewing aspect of myself . . . my essence.